CW00820938

THE SECRET LIVES OF TAYLOR SWIFT'S CATS

About the Author

Sue Chef is the long-standing music critic of the *Sandford Citizen* and one of the area's foremost cat whisperers. This is her first book.

THE SECRET LIVES OF TAYLOR SWIFT'S CATS

Sue Chef

WILDFIRE

First published in 2024 by Wildfire
An imprint of Headline Publishing Group Limited

1

Cataloguing in Publication Data is available from the British Library

Hardback ISBN 9781035427314
ebook ISBN 9781035427321

Typeset in 13/16pt CentSchbook BT by Jouve (UK), Milton Keynes

Printed and bound in Great Britain by Clays Ltd, Elcograf S.p.A.

MIX
Paper | Supporting
responsible forestry
FSC® C104740

Headline's policy is to use papers that are natural, renewable and recyclable
products and made from wood grown in well-managed forests and other
controlled sources. The logging and manufacturing processes are expected
to conform to the environmental regulations of the country of origin.

HEADLINE PUBLISHING GROUP
An Hachette UK Company
Carmelite House
50 Victoria Embankment
London EC4Y 0DZ

www.headline.co.uk
www.hachette.co.uk

This one goes out to my Day Ones, the two people who always believed in me and would never let me give up on my dream of one day writing a book about the secret lives of Taylor Swift's cats. To my parents, Ed and Little, this one's for you.

Sue Chef, July 2024

Disclaimer

The following is our version of events. Any resemblance to reality is pure coincidence.

Contents

Foreword

In this world, the only things that are certain are death and taxes.

That is, unless you're a cat. And especially if you're Taylor Swift's cat.

OK, there aren't *no* deaths (though there are certainly more lives) and I guess that *technically* there are no taxes – it's not like it's us who's paying them – but who are we kidding? Everybody wants to be a cat, and if you don't, you're lying to yourself.

I'm Meredith Grey, and I know exactly what you're thinking: *How is this cat talking to me*? (Answer: a ridiculous amount of time on our paws, and access to Duolingo Premium.) But I know what else you're thinking too: that my younger siblings – Olivia Benson and Benjamin Button – and I are the kinds of ultra-privileged, ultra-pampered, ultra-Instagrammed celebrity cats that are ultimately no use to anyone or anything. (You're not entirely wrong.)

For too long, we've hidden in the shadows, relegated to the occasional search-engine-friendly news article. But in fact, we were right in the middle of Taylor's rise to fame and world domination. And now it's time to set the record straight.

Over the course of the next few chapters, we the Mob (**M**eredith, **O**livia, **B**enjamin; Taylor learned how to do Easter eggs from us, you know) present our own version of events: of how a random ragdoll and two increasingly immobile Scottish Folds formed a firm of fixers that facilitated the far-fetched fdreams of Ftaylor Fwift, all recalled to Sandford's finest Swiftie, Sue Chef.

I believe it was Christopher Marlowe who said, 'All the world's a stage, and all the men and women merely players.' (Does that make cats the directors? I never went to drama school.) Anyway, in the all-singing, all-dancing

Swift production, I, Meredith Grey, cast myself as the don, the matriarch, the alpha overseeing a career without omega.

And sure, I *guess* the musicians, producers, management, family, Squad, the post-Squad Squad, written media and social media all helped build the Taylor we know and love in their own unique ways – not forgetting the small matter of the hundreds of millions of fans who bought records, the many more who streamed or watched the 152-show, 21-month, globe-trotting phenomenon that was the Eras Tour, and the global populace who sought to anoint a new kind of megastar for the twenty-first century – but mostly it was me.

But who were the *real* constants in her life all this time? 'I'm going to go hang out with my friends, and then I go home to the cats,' Taylor told a reporter on the Grammys red carpet in 2015. Steady and unmoving then, steadier and unmovinger today.

Overseeing Taylor's burgeoning career is no easy work, but before we begin, it would be remiss of me to not pay tribute to those no longer with us, the pets who did the groundwork for us and Taylor, even if they knew nothing of it at the time.

In the beginning, there was Indy, an adorable Siamese–tabby mix. Taylor called up best friend Abigail Anderson, just so she could share Indy snoring down the phone. 'This is the cat that I talk to when I'm lonely or bored or happy,' Taylor told the world in 2008. We give thanks to Indy, for being the first cat in a lifetime of pet-based obsessions. (There were horses and dogs too. Unfortunately, that Taylor can't come to the phone right now; she's dead.)

Then, there was Eliehsen, another Siamese. We give thanks to Eliehsen, for having a name close enough to Alison that we can safely assume Taylor Alison Swift's pets are an extension of herself and, crucially, her artistry.

I entered the tale in 2011 and quickly realised my duty. My predecessors had done a fine job in creating the right atmosphere for a young Taylor to practise her music. But in truth, this was amateur hour. In all the drama around Taylor, she needed someone strong and reliable to take care of *family* matters. You'll hear from my siblings later, but first, this is my version.

1

Meredith's Version

25 September 2008, three years before I
arrived on the scene. Taylor had known
Grey's Anatomy showrunner Shonda
Rhimes for a little while; or rather, Rhimes
had known of her. (One time, Taylor turned
up shoeless and guitarful in her office, and
proceeded to play 'Love Story' to a bemused
Rhimes while declaring her undying love
for the TV show.) So when 'White Horse'
appeared in the fifth season of *Grey's*,
something clicked for Taylor.

I entered the fold on Halloween 2011,
embodying all the characteristics expected
of a strong, independent, distinctly
unspooky TV doctor. (Despite it being the
'most important day' of Taylor's life so far, I
never really got the whole Halloween
schtick. The first and last time that Taylor

attempted to dress me and Olivia up in Halloween outfits in 2014, I tried to jump off the balcony.)

The first few months of our relationship were documented on Instagram posts painfully consigned to the pre-*Reputation* archive in the sky. But, while Olivia would later become Taylor's 'sabre-toothed tiger cub', 'baby wolverine', 'Princess of Meow Town', 'melting snowman' and 'little unicorn kitty cat', my relationship with Taylor was *far* deeper than any silly childish nicknames. The cats have had many songs over the years – see Benjamin's selection later on – but *our song* was forged from Taylor confessing to me (and only me) everything about her blossoming career, her beautiful life, her friends, her lovers and her adoring fans, and me, lying there, literally not moving a muscle, plotting all the ways I could make her dreams come true. Though missing her was dark grey, loving her was yellow. (I'm colour blind.)

Behind the scenes, things were moving

quickly. In 2012, Taylor would arrive at *Red*, an album 'about the tumultuous, crazy, insane, intense, semi-toxic relationships' she'd experienced over the past two years. (I'm not included in that, FYI.) And to help support her on that emotional journey, I needed to get organising.

THAT KOI! ALWAYS SPOILS OUR FAVOURITE PLOYS!

'Meredith is scared of the fish,' Taylor told *Vanity Fair* in March 2013, as she and a reporter toured our Nashville apartment. *Meredith is scared of the fish!* How dare she make such a provocative, reductive reading of my life, creating this two-dimensional, fictionalised cartoon of me, this jet-setting, fish-hating cat who—

OK, I lied. I was a little scared of the fish, but not quite as scared of the fish as they were of me.

I knew I could take Taylor to the top, but

I was smart enough to know I'd need minions – *family* members – to help me. Quickly, I realised that we were going to put to work the various animals in our Tim-Burton-meets-Alice-in-Wonderland-meets-Pirate-Ship-meets-Peter-Pan abode if we were going to support Taylor as she sought to bridge the gap between 'country' and 'pop with country bits in it'. The huge koi pond in the middle of the living room seemed a good place to start the recruitment drive.

Koi are generally pretty organised. You see, they swim in packs of four, to protect against predators. When they're attacked, Koi A, B and C travel in one direction, while the other one is the D koi.

Anyway, in Taylor's pond, there were not one but two families of four: the Koi family (Roy and Joy, and their sons Troy and Leroy) and the Fish family (Nish and Trish, with their daughters Eilish and the mischievous Elle).

It soon became clear that these were two

warring families of gill-bearing vertebrates; think of it as the Sharks and the Jets, or the Fish and the . . . Other Fish. Getting Eilish Fish and Troy Koi to do anything without arguing was a nigh on impossible task – they were two star-crossed lovers, divided by social class – but after a few highly choreographed street-dance routines to the music of Leonard Bernstein, I soon managed to get them back under control.

The koi were my eyes and ears, my own little secret police. Given Taylor's preference for holding any serious conversations by the pond, they were the perfect people to snoop on her personal life from just beyond the surface. But otherwise, they were useless; they just kept clicking and mumbling stuff about everything being free in America.

Taylor's birdcages had housed teenage doves, perfect for perimeter duty, but when I checked on them, the birds were gone; guess they'd flown the nest. I tried the six-foot topiary rabbit that Taylor had installed to see if he'd do a job on security for me, but he was taken aback by my offer; guess I caught him on the hop.

Things weren't working out around the house, so I gave up and snuggled into one of Taylor's many plush sofas, for a brief snooze in front of the TV.

BACK STORY

As I settled down, I leant on the remote, changed the channel and accidentally slept through the whole of *The Godfather* trilogy. I sprang from the sofa furnished with knowledge of the intricate workings of the Sicilian-American mafia structure, as well as a newfound appreciation for the cinematic art of Francis Ford Coppola. (Well, at least 66% of it.)

Over a bowl of premium Scottish salmon, I concluded that I was going to need a family structure: alongside the don (me), I would need a *consigliere*, a right-paw person to take care of 'business', and a wild card, someone out of the ordinary for special missions. And, just like in the movies, we'd also need a target: a bad guy, a good guy, a made-up guy, any kind of guy!

ALL THE MEN WE EVER MOVED

To prove their loyalty to the firm, over the years, I've assigned Mob members their own individual targets: men in Taylor's life who needed a nudge in the right direction (usually towards a trapdoor). I felt it was important to lead by example. Here are a few examples of how I consolidated power, Corleone style.

no conor, no cry

Conor Kennedy had many things going for him: dashing good looks, a famous family and, most crucially, a family mansion in Hyannis Port, Massachusetts, with premium real estate for sale next door.

Clearly, things were never going to work out with him and Taylor. (He was far too immature.) But more important than any of that love/suitability stuff was the simple fact that I was tired of Nashville.

So I got to work. Zillow alerts for properties in the Hyannis Port area were switched onto her personal email, leaving Taylor pining for the coast. 'Starlight', her song for Ethel Kennedy from years back, would mysteriously come on in the apartment at random moments. I let slip that there might be a wedding on the way between Kyle Kennedy and Liam Kerr (and we know how much Taylor loves weddings).

If this all seems a little selfish, it's because it was. Did I hurry things along slightly quicker than they ought to because I fancied feeling the sea air on my fur? Yes. Did I subtly encourage Taylor to buy the $4.8 million mansion right next to the Kennedy family complex, despite having only dated Conor for a few months, because I wanted a change of scenery? Quite possibly.

8

But would High Watch, her Rhode Island summer house that would later host her legendary Fourth of July parties and inspire 'The Last Great American Dynasty', have come about if I hadn't put myself first? Almost certainly not. Splendidly selfish, charmingly helpless – that's the Meredith Grey way.

<u>Styled Out</u>

The beach house was secured, Conor was out of the picture and, as we approached Taylor's twenty-third birthday in November 2012, everything was set. I'd shipped in twenty-three Colin the Caterpillar cakes from England, and 529 candles to go on top of them. I'd invited all the rich and famous people I could think of down to Nashville, and I'd booked Maroon 5 for the night. This was Taylor's special day: surely she'd want to spend it with her nearest, dearest, feline friend?

A week before the big day, Taylor's mood began to change; she became detached, non-committal, even stroppy with me. (Had she figured out that her brief romance with Conor had had an ulterior motive?) Then, a few days before her big celebrations, I heard the front door slam, and Taylor was gone. A hush fell over the apartment.

Her birthday came and went. All the famous people I'd invited suddenly contracted a suspiciously uniform cold, three hours before the startpoint. Feeling sorry for myself, I had no choice but to eat all the cakes, followed by all the candles, throwing up everywhere and consigning myself to my bed for the next four days. When I eventually moved out of my cat bed, I noticed that the previous day's newspaper lining the litter tray had a picture of Taylor on it, with a mystery man. On closer inspection, I saw the accompanying headline. 'Swift sits with strained smile at Harry Styles' local Chinese takeaway,' the *Daily Mail* screamed. I'd been snubbed!

Sure, maybe all children need to rebel to learn what they're missing, and perhaps they always end up back in the fold anyway. But that takeaway was a marker in our relationship. Never again would she turn me down for a Chinese in Cheshire.

At the time, Taylor loved randomly gatecrashing things she wasn't technically invited to. (Previously, she'd turned up at Conor's cousin's wedding without permission, and rather ruined the vibe – strictly speaking, the bride's mum said she wasn't invited but Taylor made clear the bride invited her.) So when she organised a Christmas ski trip with Styles – once again, without me – I thought I'd take a leaf out of her book.

Meredith Grey: Hey Tay! All packed?
Taylor Swift: I mean, I guess? I really hope Harry can *actually* ski? I don't know how much snow they get down in Cheshire.
MG: It will be *such* a romantic trip. Everything is romantic at the top of those

slopes: 360-degree views, 365 days a year? I think about it all the time.

TS: It's like the *perfect* place to fall in love.

MG: Yeah! And sharing the love is what it's all about!

TS: . . . yeah! I guess so?

MG: Going down an easy red two by two, following each other's tracks . . .

TS: Two by two?

MG: Fondue for four at the top of the slopes, hot chocolate double dates at the bottom—

TS: —wait a second . . .

MG: —and what's the one thing better than one über-successful millennial music couple on a romantic ski trip?

TS: Huh?

MG: *Two* über-successful millennial music couples on a romantic ski trip, of course!

TS: Meredith! I can't believe that you'd go behind my back like th—

MG: Relax! They're really nice, and *super* low-key – I'm sure you'll be absolutely fine, and definitely not harassed by a whole load of paparazzi for the entire time you're there, completely ruining any notions of a romantic getaway that you might have imagined.

TS: Who exactly did you invite?

MG: Justin Bieber and Selena Gomez!

The ski trip was all over every glossy magazine struggling for non-Christmas stories, and Harry couldn't take it. They separated the next month, and I returned to the centre of Taylor's life.

Having just about outlasted Harry, I was on the warpath, and so was Taylor, who came out fighting with *Red*. As well as overseeing the rise of today's foremost cultural icon, I also dabble in cultural criticism; here is a short review I wrote of *Red* that expanded on that idea of Taylor on the warpath into an incisive close read that put the text in its wider cultural context. To my surprise, none of the twenty-six publications I approached were willing to publish it.

RED

From the Mongol hordes of Genghis Khan to the Napoleonic Wars of Napoleon, war drums have been used throughout history as a kind of military Easter egg. *What's that coming over the hill?* we ask. *It is war*, they infer, though in reality, we already know.

It's in full knowledge of this tradition that Taylor begins *Red* opener 'State of Grace' with distant drums. Taylor has said many, many times that *Red* is about the different ways to say goodbye to an ex, but I for one am still convinced that it is actually about war. For starters, a deal of the album is in C major, which, according to music theorist Marc-Antoine Charpentier writing in 1712, makes music 'gay and warlike'. And really, what is the ending of any relationship but a war of some kind?

Much like the opening morning of the Battle of Agincourt, it's a little while before any action properly starts. We're four tracks in before we hear those warlike, military drums kick in once again on 'I Knew You Were Trouble', foretelling

of the Greatest War of Taylor's career to date:
the immovable object of country versus the
unstoppable object of pop.

A minute in, the bass drops; in a moment, the
dubstep genie is out of the bottle, screaming, 'Let
Battle Commence!' as he's actively wafted around
by producers Max Martin and Shellback. It's a
war, it's the fiercest fight of her life and those
darn drums started it. Nothing was ever the same
again.

Red took Taylor global; our battle
expanded, and our fixers were looking
threadbare. I needed back-up.

2

Olivia's Version

'So I got a new cat.' And the crowd. Went. Wild.

Is there anything more 2014 than announcing your new cat on *The Ellen DeGeneres Show*? *Detective* Olivia Benson here, mostly to reminisce about how we ushered in the Golden Age of Taylor Swift's Cat Branding, and partly to correct my sister on her God complex.

Ellen was in October, but I'd entered the fold a few months before. It was a bright, cold day in April, and the clocks were striking thirteen – Taylor's favourite number – as I received my tap on the shoulder at precisely 1300 hours while out at an exclusive lunch date for young singles at a venue on the Lower East Side.

A few minutes later, I was bundled into a cat box and taken to a secret location to meet Meredith. In a dark, windowless room, she presented me with her files. She was building an elite team of fixers – 'a *family*', she said, in a hideous Italian-American accent – that was going to elevate Taylor Swift to heights of global superstardom previously thought unimaginable, through a mixture of man-management and over-Easter-egged ways of describing said man-management.

MEREDITH'S OWN-BRAND EASTER EGGS, AND WHAT THEY MEAN FOR NORMAL PEOPLE

- 'We're going to make him an offer he can't refuse.' Translation: we will sit on him for a bit.
- 'It seems like there might have to be a little accident.' Translation: one of us will use his shoe as a toilet.

- 'Looks like we'll have to deal with the situation.' Translation: we will not deal with the fallout of a relationship between two consenting, emotionally mature humans, but when we eventually write the book, we will claim to have had overdue influence in the emotional lives of both our owner and her lover. (Just kidding! Love you Meredith xxx)

She'd mentioned a couple of her attempts to recruit from the immediate Swift circles had been unsuccessful – there was something about *West Side Story* that I didn't really follow – but I heard her out. We were just two normal Scottish Folds, two innocent Scottish Folds, and I liked her.

The problem was that Meredith was set in her ways. For her, 'taking care of business' meant some elaborate scheme involving ropes, pulleys, the positioning of the Earth, intense melancholy and an apple. (That's what did for Tom Hiddleston, apparently.) But here was an analogue cat working in a digital world. Not only did we need man-management, we needed *brand* management.

My hard launch, on *Ellen*, was with a shoe by Keds, an appeal to average Americans worried that a post-*Red*-and-*1989* Taylor was moving away from the Miss Americana brand. Through an intimate relationship with a producer's cat (details of which I will NOT be divulging), I later managed to get not one but *two* headline-making appearances on *The Graham Norton Show*, the most infamous being alongside actor John Cleese, who, as well as asking, 'How did *it* have the accident?' asked if I was 'a proper cat'. (Taylor has gone on to become a billionaire adored by millions worldwide, whereas Cleese has starred in critically acclaimed movies such as *Get Squirrely* and *Charlie's Angels: Full Throttle*.)

For the most part, my role as Taylor's official-unofficial-official brand consultant and media strategist was going swimmingly. I decided that the best way to promote Taylor was, of course, to promote myself. (The world's most successful autocracies are built on having family members in important positions.) I was appearing in commercials and music videos, on Instagram, Twitter and Vine, and Taylor was doing pretty well too.

Then someone came along who looked like my next mistake.

FOREVER & ALWYN?

Joe was . . . a difficult one. He was also kind of my idea.

2016 was a dark time for Taylor: the end of her relationship with Calvin Harris, and the short-lived romance with Hiddleston featuring *that* T-shirt. There was also the Kanye debacle over the use of the word 'bitch' in his single 'Famous', the Kim Kardashian Snapchat drama soon after, and the public humiliation that followed when an edited tape emerged that appeared to catch Taylor red-handed. (The truth would out, but not for a long while.)

'I felt alone, I felt really bitter,' she would later explain on *Miss Americana*. 'I felt sort of like a wounded animal lashing out. I figured I had to reset everything. I had to reconstruct an entire belief system for my own personal sanity.' The only thing I could do from my perspective was offer a *brand* reset. Harris-Swift sounded like an insurance company, Hiddleswift was . . . disgusting. We needed uncombinable, something more low-key, something less . . . *brandable*?

Joe Alwyn, a man whose name couldn't possibly be collapsed into Taylor's, was perfect.

With Joe came heart-throb good looks, a calm demeanour, a family tree that included the British composers Doreen Carwithen and William Alwyn, and, of course, London and all its songwriting potential. In the time after the Kanye stuff, there was a complete creative rebrand. The anger of *Reputation* – including the torching of all our photos from her Instagram, without explanation – was extinguished in a single gesture: the snake in the 'ME!' video, so indicative of the ongoing Kimye feud, exploded into flowers.

At the time, things seemed to be finally settling down, from my perspective at least. I was living the jet-set lifestyle between Nashville, New York and London, trying out a range of the world's best cat carriers.

CAT CARRIERS: A RANKING, BY OLIVIA BENSON

- The Holdall (aka Jim Class-Hero): Ah, Jim. We love you dearly, so much that we actually had a name for you, but society has progressed past the need for a transporter that looks how Jake Gyllenhaal (reportedly) smells. Pros:

N/A. Cons: cramped, sweaty, was once mistaken for an actual gym bag and taken to a 6 a.m. spin class.

- The Catpack (aka The Over the Shoulder Smoulder Holder): This little leather contraption with a cute Perspex viewing window gives us pout-perfect travel in permanent rear-view. Pros: good for reminiscing (always facing backwards). Cons: poor ventilation.
- By Hand: Truly the most Main Character way to travel. Pros: GREAT ventilation. Cons: paparazzi-friendly.
- The Stella McCartney Cat Carrier: A total vibe. Luxurious, discreet, admittedly slightly coffin-like. Pros: can nap without shame. Cons: makes me want my life outfitted by SM, which is financially dangerous.

Meredith seemed happy enough with what I was up to, so long as I couched all my activities in barely discernible gangsterish metaphors. On paper, Taylor ended up in her longest ever relationship; things were settled, quiet and even looking to the future. Was 'Lover' her paean to Joe, someone she had known for twenty seconds that felt like twenty years? Was 'Paper Rings' her anti-consumerist song dropping big hints about a proposal? None of this was ever confirmed, but with Taylor and Joe as parents, and Benjamin coming into the fray, we did begin to feel like an actual family, not just one of the ones that Meredith dreamt up.

Yet looking back today, this Era was just as tricky as any other.

LONDON BORE

Taylor's relationship with London has been thoroughly dissected in the media. Her move to the capital successfully anglified her brand, hitting the UK market hard and fast. But it also brought about some of her worst songwriting, not least in the

reprehensible 'London Boy'. Here's what
I mean:

- 'I enjoy walking Camden Market
  in the afternoon.' This is a lie. Nobody
  likes walking in Camden Market *at
  any time*, especially not in the
  afternoon.

- 'Took me back to Highgate, met all of his
  best mates.' All of them had names that
  ended in 'ie' or 'y': Jamie, Ollie, Stevie,
  Smithy, Chuggsy (?) and, ironically,
  Swiftie, who reverted back to his first
  name, Jonathan, in Taylor's company.
  Though they were nice enough to me,
  Alwyn's conversations with friends were
  always so dull; why immortalise them
  in song?

- 'I enjoy nights in Brixton, Shoreditch in
  the afternoon.' I'm not saying that Taylor
  Swift name-dropping these
  neighbourhoods further accelerated
  London's housing crisis, but I'm not *not*
  saying that either.

- 'So please show me Hackney / Doesn't have to be Louis V up on Bond Street.' To be fair, this one checks out: famously, the only two things worth doing in London are 1) spending any remaining disposable income you might have accrued on expensive clothes that you don't need, and 2) going to Columbia Road Flower Market.

Thank the Lord she said so long to her London phase, eh?

There were other signs that things were going a bit Pete Tong, as I believe Cockneys say. Taylor had always dreamt of a future on-stage; she once died in Eddie Redmayne's arms during an audition for *Les Misérables*, for God's sake. So when she told me she was in a new film, I was lost for words. The conversation went a little bit like this:

Taylor Swift: Olivia, my Dibbles, my wolverine, my Princess of Meow Town! I have something super-exciting to tell you!

Olivia Benson: [quizzically] Miaow?!

TS: I've had a call with Tom Hooper and I'm going to be in a new film!

OB: [excitedly] Miaow!

TS: And it's got Idris Elba in it! And Judi Dench, and Francesca Hayward, and Jennifer Hudson—

OB: [more excitedly] Miaow!!!

TS: —and James Corden!

OB: [significantly less excitedly] Miaow.

TS: And it's with Andrew Lloyd Webber, and it's *Cats*, and you're going to love it! So the premise of it is there are a whole bunch of humans playing cats, and there's loads of CGI involved that blurs the distinctions between cat and human—

OB: [nervously] Miaow?

TS: —and Judi Dench wears a fur coat despite being a cat, and Rebel Wilson peels off a layer of cat to reveal another layer of cat, and we all have human toes despite being cats, and we're all really small, and some of us are inexplicably sexy—

OB: [even more nervously] Miaow?! Miaow?!

TS: —and I'm going to play Bombalurina and sing 'Macavity' while descending from a great big moon in the sky and sprinkling catnip everywhere—

OB: [intensely alarmed] Miaow?!?!

TS: —and I'm doing this because I *love* you, and I want to be more *in touch* with you, and Joe also said he liked the idea and he'd back me on it, but it's mostly because I *adore* you and your sister! Anyway, I'm going away to cat school next month to learn how to be a cat for a few days and it might turn into a few weeks or a few months, who knows? Bye!

It was a disaster. The critics baulked at this profoundly disturbing film, and there was little any of us could do other than watch the negative reviews sail in.

Meredith was furious with me; I'd let her down, I'd let myself down, and most importantly of all, I'd let Taylor down. She said that too much focus on brand management had opened Taylor up to this kind of fall. My excuse – that, in the shock of this career pivot, I momentarily forgot how to communicate past a single word – fell on deaf ears.

Things with Joe became sort of unmanageable – how can you be a brand consultant to a brand that refuses to be a brand? – but Meredith kept on nagging me, searching for somebody to do some 'old-fashioned man-management' as her own health began to decline. Eventually, I caved by creating a man all of my own.

A BETTER MAN: NILS SJÖBERG

'VERY STOKED about this cover of lwymmd on @KillingEve by Jack leopards & the dolphin club!!' Taylor tweeted in May 2020. 'Look What You Made Me Do' was already dripping with subtext before this moment; with a whole load of snakes in the promo run, and lyrics that fired a blanket round at enemies plural, Taylor had been responding, fiercely, to the dramatic events of 2016.

There couldn't be a better place to release the single than 'Beautiful Monster', an episode of *Killing Eve* where Villanelle, Hélène and Eve deal with the essentially Swiftian conundrum of chasing one's desires, then getting your fingers burned, then kind of enjoying that pain. 'Do you know why I love you, Villanelle?' Hélène says at one point. 'Because you're an agent of chaos and I love chaos.' With Leopards' new husky vocals, it's almost as if the track is purring along.

The setting was flawless; the pitch, perfect. The trouble – or the genius – was that neither Jack Leopards nor The Dolphin Club nor their co-writer, Nils Sjöberg, actually ever existed. It was all Taylor, or as I can now exclusively reveal, her cats' idea.

As terminally online people – what is a twenty-first century fixer for an international pop superstar without a small army of burner accounts? – Meredith and I knew how accusations of industry plants clung to anyone suspiciously new around these parts.

Enter stage left: a mysterious Swedish songwriter, with a songwriting knack bearing an uncanny resemblance to one Taylor Alison Swift. Could he be a decoy?

To get rid of a man is easy enough, but to *create* a man anew is a whole different ball game. You need three things. First, a plain-sight disguise: Nils, the most popular male first name in Sweden, meets Sjöberg, the most popular surname in Sweden. Second, a motive. That one was easy – a mysterious Swedish man directs attention away from Taylor, allowing her songwriting to shine on its own merits (and to avoid any flak from the misjudged *Cats*). Third, cover: Lewis Capaldi wrote songs for other artists under the name Sooka Phatwan; why not do the same here, but more subtly?

The plan was simple: write songs for other artists undercover, create a Nils extended universe, and let Taylor carry on creating undeterred by questions like 'Which boyfriend is this one about?' And it worked, for the most part. *Hannah Montana*, Boys Like Girls and even the 'Nothin' on You' rapper B.o.B benefitted from the sly Swede's songwriting.

Then, disaster struck. 'Nils' wrote 'This Is What You Came For' with Taylor's former boyfriend Calvin Harris, who almost gave the game away, all but revealing his true identity and forcing Taylor to pull the plug on Nils. (Just to be on the safe side, I made sure Harris knew what side of the bread Taylor's toast was buttered on with a text from a burner phone reminding him of an interview he'd given to *ShortList* in 2009, in which he revealed that he'd chosen the pseudonym Calvin Harris because it sounded 'a bit racially ambiguous'.)

By that point, Nils was long gone, but if it's one thing we are, it's thorough. Look again at the 'Look What You Made Me Do' video, the bit where Taylor digs her way out of her own grave, and there, on a chunky headstone, is the name *Nils Sjöberg*.

RIP in peace, Mr Sjöberg. You were good fun while you lasted.

Something Meredith won't tell you is why exactly we're close. She might be more *man*-management, and I might be more *brand* management, but both of us are Scottish Folds of a certain age, and neither of us is getting younger.

Though she tries not to show it, Meredith's role in the Mob these days involves less and less time in the field. I feel the effects of osteochondrodysplasia less profoundly than she does, but there's a certain irony in the fact that the condition that causes our ears to flop forward in a cutesy kind of way also ensures that we have a lifetime of joint pain, bone deficiencies and arthritis. Our fame has spread so far that experts are actively lobbying for Swifties – or any other people for that matter – not to buy our breed.

Meredith would never say this out loud, but our Era has an endpoint.

Meanwhile, Taylor returned from *Cats* a changed woman. She would scamper about the house, grooming herself and pretending to cough up furballs. She would lick milk directly from the bowl Ian McKellen-style, and one time, in a fit of rage, she clawed her way through an entire designer sofa. It was clear that she had an idea about what cats *should* be. And that just wasn't the brand journey Meredith and I were on.

As Taylor accelerated into her next Era, she needed somebody energetic: a maverick, willing to do things a bit differently . . .

3

Benjamin's Version

. . . So this one time I like joined this cult . . . it's called like the Mob – bit naff imo – but anyway I'm in it and then a massive pandemic happens and I'm like *eek no thank you* but then Taylor releases *folklore/evermore* and I'm really much more of a *folklore/evermore* girlie than a *Lover* girli—

You sly dog! You caught me monologuing! Let's clear one thing up straight away: that is *not* the real me. Benjamin Button, Esq., is not the airy, bundle-of-fun, Gen-Z cat that everyone expects, but in fact an actor, classically trained, and of some repute. And from the moment I was presented to the world from the inside lining of Brendon Urie's flowery suit jacket, my destiny – as a star of screen and stage – was confirmed.

But unlike my darling older sisters, I had to *hustle*.

2019: I was abandoned by my owners and picked up by an agency that put cats in commercials, in the hope somebody might adopt them. We had all sorts at our adoption centre: TV extras chewed up and spat out by the Hollywood machine; old A-list Santa Monica pets whose breeds had since gone out of fashion; a tabby who was the perfect handbag cat, until handbags got too small.

Life inside was a dull cycle of fleeting hope, crushed excruciatingly slowly by reality. Cats were selected first thing in the morning, whisked away to some random shoot, hoping to catch an eye on set. If they didn't, they'd return to the cattery in the early hours and spend the next few weeks praying that some warm-hearted cable viewer watching late-night commercials for toothpaste or fabric softener might fall in love with them. They rarely did.

Usually, selection was a random process – a handler would swing the door of the cattery and scoop up whoever looked keenest – but there were whispers about the 'ME!' shoot for weeks before it happened. I allowed myself to dream; Taylor, a cat-lover, shooting a video featuring cats, which would go out to her legion of fans, many of whom are cat-lovers? Others were more sceptical – 'What might Taylor Swift want with *another* cat,' a Burmese I recognised from a dry-food ad scoffed. 'We're past the Era for cats,' a sedentary Persian added. 'That was soooo three years ago.'

So when the handler came the morning of the shoot, I practically jumped into her arms, unopposed.

I'd cut my teeth on the commercial adoption circuit, and when you're in that situation, every second counts: every roll, every purr, every random 'wander' onto the set has to be micromanaged in order to maximise exposure. 'He's a little purr machine,' Taylor told the handler in a break between filming. Too right she was; I'd been practising my purring for three hours a day.

Taylor's jaw dropped when she found out I was available. The deal was done swiftly, and my life was changed, but the nagging feeling that I'd overdone it a little wouldn't shift. 'I've never met a cat that loves people so much,' Taylor enthused to Brendon, as she cooed over me and rubbed my belly. I do love *certain* people – rich actors, mostly – but I'm not the most naturally gregarious type. She took me back, dressed me up in cute clothes and called me – of all things! – Benjamin Button, condemning me to a lifetime growing ever-more immature.

I'd got the part, but at what cost?

Joining the Mob was kind of a non-negotiable at that point. Meredith sat me down and explained that she was building an elite team of fixers – 'a *family*,' she said, in a hideous Italian-American accent – that was going to elevate Taylor Swift to heights of global superstardom previously thought unimaginable. (I had a

feeling she'd made this speech before.)
Meredith wanted me as her maverick
capo, the one person in her slightly
bizarre cat-mafia structure who was given
free rein to make decisions as he saw fit,
but I'd need to prove myself. (More on
that later.)

And yet it felt like I'd arrived at a party
that was already dying down. Joe was
fiiiiine, and, more to the point, he loved us.
If ever we needed some attention, he could
quite easily be convinced to cryptically post
a photo of one of us looking cute – usually
me – on Instagram. (That became a two-
birds-one-stone arrangement; it would give
the bare minimum to fans wishing to pry
into a relationship both parties were
determined to keep private, while increasing
our public brand. Plus, the camera *loves*
me.) Meanwhile, albums tumbled out of
Taylor in lockdown, and *evermore* quickly
followed *folklore*. While everyone else was
baking banana breads and doing Zoom
quizzes, Taylor was quietly getting on

41

with making that period's defining
soundtrack.

When you are young they assume you
know nothing, and, generally, I did have a
marvellous time ruining everything.
Occasionally that was immortalised in
song . . .

LOOK HOW THEY MASSACRED
MY TOY

During Covid when I was wandering
around the apartment in my usual Benji
fashion, I found my favourite toy horse . . .

And I truly and honestly didn't believe
that I was going to break it and I swear
the only thing I did was chew lightly on his
antique head, but with a fat snap, head
and torso were no longer together and the
body lay motionless on the floor as the
horse's head poked out of my mouth.

And I panicked and rushed into Taylor's
bedroom to try to hide the evidence and

that's how Taylor Swift ended up with a horse's head in her bed.

And eventually Taylor found the body and the head and then me.

'Oh sweetie,' she soothed. 'It seems you've bitten off a bit more than you can chew.'

And then it dawned on her that there might be a metaphor in that, and now we have 'My Boy Only Breaks His Favorite Toys' and it might be a bit about . . . me?

I still had to prove myself, and I did it the only way I knew how: through general luvvy-ish schmoozing. Like I mentioned before, on the commercial adoption circuit, every second counts, and I'd worked my way into the hearts – and the phone books – of many A-listers. One of those was famed cat-lover Kelly Clarkson. In July 2019, I decided to send her a quick message:

Hi Kelly C! Hope all is well with you. Heard you've got a new show – congrats! Is it true that you've got The Rock on first up?! Mega! Listen, could you do me a big *huge massive favour? I've just been adopted by Taylor Swift!!!! (How exciting!!!!!!) Anyway, she's having some difficulties with obtaining her masters at the moment, and is a *teensy* bit stuck with what to do next. I was wondering, could you do me a big huge massive favour and tweet something like:*

'Just a thought, U should go in & re-record all the songs that U don't own the masters on exactly how U did them but put brand new art & some kind of incentive so fans will no longer buy the old versions. I'd buy all of the new versions just to prove a point'?

Maybe put an emoji on the end just to make sure it's your own work? (Will mean so much more coming from you.) And if you could send it late at night UK time so that it's the last thing she sees before she goes to bed and will maybe dream about it? Thanks a MILLION, drinks soon xxx

She did it, and lo, the Versions Era was born.

But, with lockdown thoroughly set in, and the promise of Taylor's world domination imminent (on top of the

Versions project, there was still *Midnights* to come, even before the Eras Tour and *The Tortured Poets Department*), there was little for me to do. I spent a lot of time on Reddit – for character work, I swear – familiarising myself with the lore, and even writing some of my own. . .

FIVE SONGS THAT, WHILE UNCONFIRMED, ARE DEFINITELY 100% ABOUT MEREDITH GREY, OLIVIA BENSON AND BENJAMIN BUTTON, BY U/BENJAMINBUTTON

- 'This Is Why We Can't Have Nice Things': A regular joke that Taylor makes around the house that, as cats, we have no way of rolling our eyes at.
- 'I Look in People's Windows': I'm pretty sure we all agree that, in this song, Taylor catches glances at other cats in secret so as not to make us feel jealous. Back me up on this one, guys?

- 'You Need to Calm Down': I literally don't, but whatever.

- 'I Did Something Bad': So this dates from at least two years before I was born but it definitely speaks to the time that I threw up in Ed Sheeran's shoe right before a performance and he didn't notice until he stomped on his loop pedal.

- 'Death by a Thousand Cuts': More like LIFE by a thousand CATS, right?

ALTERNATIVE NAMES FOR BENJAMIN BUTTON THAT ARE LESS LIKELY TO FORCE HIM INTO A CREATIVE DEAD-END AND INSTEAD ARE INSPIRED BY TAYLOR LYRICS, BY U/MENJAMINMUTTON

- *Tim*, as in McGraw, the early boyfriend responsible for the world's greatest opening line to a discography!

- *Peter*, as in 'Cardigan'/Joe Alwyn/Matty Healy?

- *Cornelius*, as in the gender-flipped street, obviously.

- *Romeo*, as in Christopher Marlowe's *Romeo and Juliet*, which was, I believe, based on Taylor's song 'Love Story'.

- *Walthamstow*, as in the location on a now-deleted version of 'London Boy'.

When I wasn't wasting time, I was killing time. By September 2023, I'd bided my time and that time was up. (It was full time.) The time had come. It was time to face the music. This was my time.

ME! TIME!

The first thing to say about the *Time* magazine cover which I star in – as the (unofficial) Cat of the Year, the first feline since the pharaohs to be bestowed with such an honour – is that it was not my decision to feature ahead of my siblings, despite undoubtedly being the most deserving. Mine was the true rags-to-riches tale, though wisely, little of that made it into Taylor's cover interview. (This was her moment as well as mine.)

And yet I was conscious that I was living out other cats' dreams. Meredith, with her corny accents, her belief in bureaucracy and her obfuscatory metaphors, had been in this game for years, largely without reward (except for regular portions of premium Scottish salmon). Olivia, the media darling, who had put in the hard yards doing advertisements for Diet Coke and AT&T, who ended up on a T-shirt in the *Deadpool* movie, who was so obsessed with branding and image that it got in the way of a common-sense decision not to star in *Cats*, would have loved to have been on that cover.

When it was finally released, Taylor tweeted:

Time Magazine: We'd like to name you Person of the Yea-
Me: Can I bring my cat.

My cat. Not *one* of my cats. Not plain old
Benjamin, but *my* cat. I felt more than a
little smug, but I returned to the Mob
embarrassed at what had gone on.

It was a difficult time for the three of us.
By this point, Meredith was less and less
mobile, and Olivia was starting to feel the
impact. We had had five world-beating
years as a trio, but I wasn't sure if it might
be the end of the road. I genuinely
wondered if I might be best running away
from home. But before I made my decision,
there was just one more thing . . .

PLEASE, I'VE FALLEN FOR DENISE, CHANGE THE PROPHECY

They say love is like the offside rule in
football: impossible to explain, but you
know it when you see it. And from the

moment I first locked eyes on her (as Joe flicked through endless English TV channels in their London flat one early evening), I knew. I was literally *obsessed*. Her hair, her skin, her face; her mannerisms, the way she *flirted* with everyone; the way she carried on with her life regardless of what anyone thought (for the most part).

For in that moment I had fallen head over heels in love with Ms Denise Welch.

Denise, for those of you foolish enough not to know, is a British actress and television personality. I fell for her portrayal of Steph Haydock, the unlucky-in-love, murderously camp French teacher in UK high school drama *Waterloo Road*, but I could quite easily have fallen for her in Northern cop thriller *Spender*, in *Corrie* or *Hollyoaks*, or as a regular commentator on my favourite mid-morning UK chat show, *Loose Women*.

There's a lot that Taylor and Denise have in common: tabloids hang off their every word, they were both into capes in 2016, and some other things I've forgotten right at this moment. But when I found out that she had a son who was hot, in a band and kind of problematic, and that Taylor *already knew* him, I saw my opportunity. Matty Healy was my Conor Kennedy, my moment to finally get what *I* really wanted.

Listening to early drafts of *Midnights* I innocently suggested that maybe what it needed was something new and alternative, a different flavour, like Sex, Chocolate or Money! 'Aren't those just names of songs by The 1975?' Taylor replied. The songwriting sessions with Swift and Healy began.

Things slowly moved into place, and eventually, Taylor met Denise after she performed at a 1975 concert in January 2023, posing for smug, satisfied backstage photos as I watched on from the sofa. (I'd never told Taylor anything about the strength of my feelings towards Denise, but my plan was unfolding perfectly.)

So, to get him out of the picture for a

while, I organised a fake month-long 'free-thinking' podcast festival in Singapore, featuring all his favourite men, and sent him an invitation to headline. He accepted immediately. With Matty not around, and cat-sitting duties still to contend with, I hoped that the chronically disorganised Healy would ask Denise to cover for him.

Just as you can't spell awesome without me, you can't spell Benjamin Button without a but. Denise was simply too busy being a Loose Woman to contend with a month of round-the-clock care, and instead, Matty sent his dad, *Benidorm*'s Tim Healy, in his place.

It all ended in tears for me and Denise, but at least there was a silver lining for the Mob: while in Singapore, Matty 'found himself' and decided that the relationship could go no further.

P.S. Denise, if you're reading this: This one is about you. You know who you are. I love you.

4

The Mob's Version (by Meredith)

Let's get a couple things straight. No
matter whose account you read, no
matter which 'experts' you listen to,
no matter how much you haven't seen
me on Instagram, Twitter, X or any of
that stuff, I am still the boss around here.
I may not move as much as I used to –
some days, I hardly move at all – but
there's still a chain of command around
this place and the buck stops with me.
Period.

Though Benjamin dealt valiantly, if
bizarrely, with the joker in the pack – Matty
Healy – I know what you're thinking:
Whatever happened to Taylor and Joe? The
answer? Our most ingenious mission yet:
Operation Fizzling Out.

THIS IS US TRYING

If anything, it was too settled. Taylor and Joe seemed to be happily, quietly, undramatically getting on with their lives in the privacy of their various London flats, Taylor writing album after album then heading out on tour (Covid permitting), Joe building his acting career and contributing cute little co-writes to Taylor albums under the pseudonym William Bowery.

This was lovely, but it put the Mob in a tricky situation. Anxious thoughts started to accumulate: What future was there for our team if Taylor wasn't constantly moving forward? What would happen to the fixers if there was nothing to fix?

What made it even harder was that there wasn't a clear ending for Taylor and Joe: no chance of an end-all phone call out of the blue, no weird comments on a podcast, no accidental revealing of a meticulously prepared alter ego, no nothing.

So we devised Operation Fizzling Out, a series of subtle tweaks to Taylor and Joe's tranquil everyday lives that created the illusion that the relationship might be ending of its own accord. Little did they know, it was actually three mischievous Mob members pulling the strings in the background.

- First, the central heating of their flat would go really hot, then really cold, then really hot again. (So as to avoid detection, we limited these episodes to every three hours on every day with a 'u' in it.) After a few weeks, Taylor would notice the temperature changes, and quietly blame Joe for it.

- Then, we'd swap the smaller and larger bowls in the dishwasher, occasionally throwing the odd plate in there to switch things up.

- On weekends, the TV volume would be 'mysteriously' left on either 12 or 14, instead of Taylor's lucky 13.

- Finally, during the week, we put together a detailed snoring rota. Working in twos, one of us would play snoring sounds using an online snoring simulator, while the other would wake one of them up, alternating through the week. Neither snored, and yet both accused each other. Sure, these tweaks were delicate, but delicately genius.

These days, cats stop me in the street to congratulate me about Taylor's monumental recent success. They ask me, 'How did you do it?' Talk to Benjamin, and he'll tell you that his *Time* cover was the moment that we won – a moment where brand met reality, where the backroom became the front room, and where the structure was made flesh: the word made fur.

Speak to Olivia, and she'll say it was won much earlier. She might have ultimately messed up with the Joe Alwyn thing – what happened back there nobody else will ever know – but, by helping him stay in the room at a time when Taylor was at her most vulnerable, it meant a true reset of *everything* could occur. Would the world domination of *Midnights* or the globe-trotting Eras Tour have happened without Olivia making a shrewd business decision to plump for a guy with a name unsuitable to portmanteau? I'm not so sure. Taylor needed to be her own woman, and Olivia gave her that chance.

Me? I think it was won long before that. It was in the moment that a young girl picked up her first guitar with a Nashville computer repair man who taught her to strum her first few chords, and then let her be. Let us take a final moment to remember the unsung hero in all of this: Taylor Alison Swift herself.

5

Sue's Version

It's 6 a.m. Sandford time when Meredith, Olivia and Benjamin – plus their unusually quiet publicist, Tassie Turn – jump on a video call with me from their home on the East Coast.

The atmosphere is frosty. It's clear that, in the time between our conversations, the Mob has read what the others have had to say, and not all of it has gone down well.

Each cat told me their stories in enormous amounts of detail. But as your loyal Mob correspondent – and as the *Citizen*'s lead music journalist for the past thirteen years – I felt it my professional duty to tie up a couple of loose ends with Meredith, Olivia and Benjamin.

What I didn't expect was the unravelling of the entire enterprise . . .

Sue Chef: Thanks so much for joining me here today! Can you all hear me OK?

Benjamin Button: Yes, no, absolutely!

Olivia Benson: Yes, I can hear you, Sue Chef.

Meredith Grey: [stares, unblinkingly]

SC: Uh, great! So, I'd like to start by asking how much you *all* have *been* en-*joying* the *Eras Tour*??!!

MG: Well, yes, naturally. It is the logical extension of exactly what we'd been planning for years. Taylor Swift has not ascended as much as sublimated; from her solid form as *the* popular music sensation of the past decade, she has become a gaseous state that is as much part of us as she is around us. She is more than oxygen; she's like a vapour, a mist on a crisp spring morning. Those of us who have been breathing in Taylor for years know precisely what that feels like. [laughs] So I guess . . . it's nice for it to be shared around.

BB: Yeah . . . I would second all of that, but add that I loved her 'Vigilante Sh*t' the most. That one rocks! Plus, the track speaks deeply to my personal experience of being a vigilante who is really bad at their job.

MG: I never cared for that track.

OB: Wait, but didn't you—

MG: Personally manipulate it so that 'Vigilante Sh*t' was announced live on TikTok with me in the corner of the shot, generating headlines in the press noting the first time she had used a curse word in a title, while ensuring that I, Meredith Grey, remained in my natural place, front and centre of the action—

OB: Wait, wha—

MG: —in order to ensure that cats remained an essential part of the Taylor Swift brand? Of course! It was a business move, darling! Chill out . . .

BB: *Je suis calme!!*

[There's a brief silence, and everyone looks at each other.]

SC: Uh, anyway . . . so, what was the reason for deciding to tell your version – or versions – of the story right now? You're all cats with net worths in tens of millions of dollars. Surely you must be looking for something other than the pay cheque?

OB: Well, I think *Meredith* can answer that one.

BB: Yeah, go on *Meredith*, you always seem to have Something To Say.

MG: Well, I . . . [She stumbles for a second, before regaining control.] It was a group decision that we, as a *family*, took to ensure that, in the long run, our significant contributions to the global rise of Taylor Swift were remembered as more than a colourful footnote. It's for the historical record, more than anything. This book's conclusion is simple: it says in big bold letters that It. Was. Us.

Tassie Turn: I think that's a good place to wrap up, Sue! Thanks ever so much for your—

OB: But that's not the *only* reason we're here though, is it, Meredith?

BB: Yeah, *isn't* it, *Me-re-dith*?

[There's a longer silence this time, and after a few long seconds, Meredith begins to speak, a little quieter than before.]

MG: Things were so great. Like, *so* great. We had our merch ranges, appeared in adverts, we were constantly on Instagram or referenced on Twitter, we were a fixture of the kinds of easy, breakfast TV slots where cat-talk is *purrfect*. [OB rolls her eyes, unsuccessfully.] People were *obsessed* with us . . .

OB: . . . and sure, it changed a little bit over time as Taylor got bigger, and there were more people vying for her time, which is *fine*, and so our role changed to a more facilitative, backroom role . . .

MG: But then *Reputation* happened and *boom*, the Instagram posts of us came down, and there were all these snakes, and grit, and *sexiness* in their place, which is *fine*, but it seemed like the start of an Era that we weren't part of . . .

BB: Don't get me wrong, there were moments. There were always moments – the pandemic being one, the *Lover* era, my *Time* cover being another [MG and OB roll their eyes, again unsuccessfully] where we really felt part of something again, but with Taylor now being away so much, and us being home a lot because of health and travel restrictions . . .

MG: She is truly like a mist. You can feel her presence if you reach slowly and carefully, but nowadays, you can never truly hold her, like she used to hold us . . .

[In a feat I believe to be medically impossible, Meredith sheds a single tear.]

OB: Everyone always asks how the Eras Tour has been for us, knowing we paved the way for it. But now it's nearly over, and I don't think—

MB: *We* don't think—

BB: We don't *know* what happens next,
for our star who has conquered the world.
It's much easier to reminisce about the
certainties of the past, rather than
imagining a future that's scary and
uncertain. That way, you sort of age in
reverse. (I should know; I'm *literally* named
after Benjamin Button.)

OB: There's a famous passage that I'm
often drawn to when asked to describe what
I think Taylor is going through right now:
'And when Alexander saw the breadth of his
domain, he wept, for there were no more
worlds left to conquer.'

BB: Neat quote! Where's it from?

OB: *Die Hard*!

SC: Benjamin, you mention the future . . .
What with Swift's global dominance, and
Travis Kelce around – who seems like a
lovely guy – and the success of the Eras
Tour, and, I mean, it's not like any of you
are getting any younger . . .

OB: What exactly are you trying to say?

BB: Yeah, *spit it out*, Chef!

SC: I . . . What I meant was . . . You guys are Taylor's fixers. But what happens to the fixers when everything seems . . . fixed?

[The screen freezes. Meredith, Olivia and Benjamin do not return.]

More Humour Titles Available from Wildfire

WILDFIRE

The Downing Street Guide to Party Etiquette
By
Verity Bigg-Knight

Partygate? More like party GREAT!

While the UK locked down to prevent
the spread of COVID-19, Boris Johnson's Number
Ten played host to a series of boozy shindigs.
Now, for the first time, you can learn to get
wasted like they do in Whitehall. The Downing
Street Party Guide will take you through every
stage of a successful, pandemic-defying bash,
from drafting invitations to answering
awkward questions later.

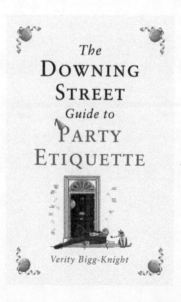

Elon Musk (Almost) Saves The World
By
Lucien Young

**The world's richest man faces the
galaxy's deadliest threat!** Everyone's favourite
billionaire makes his pulse-pounding debut in
this rip-roaring sci-fi adventure.

When an ALIEN ARMADA menaces our
planet, Earth's governments and armed
forces find themselves powerless to resist.
In desperation, humanity turns to one man:
billionaire, futurist and Twitter addict
ELON MUSK.

Trump: The Prison Diaries
By
Lucien Young

In this explosive first-person account of
swapping the White House for the Big House,
Donald Trump aims to **Make Prison
Great Again.**

Trump: The Prison Diaries is a satirical
riot – The Apprentice meets The Shawshank
Redemption. So brace yourself, because
orange is the new orange.

Kim Jong-Fun: Party Hard the
North Korean Way
By
Respected Comrade Kim Jong Un

LOYAL COMRADES to PUT THE 'PARTY' IN 'WORKERS' PARTY OF KOREA'!

For the baby-faced dictator in your life, a guide
to throwing shindigs that go off like an
intercontinental ballistic missile.

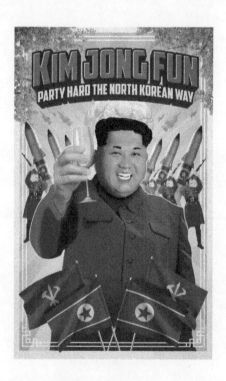